100 Things I'm Not Going to Do Now That I'm Over 50

Wendy Reid Crisp

A Perigee Book

THE BERKLEY PUBLISHING GROUP
Published by the Penguin Group
Penguin Group (USA) Inc.
375 Hudson Street, New York, New York 10014, USA
Penguin Group (Canada), 90 Eglinton Avenue East, Suite 700, Toronto, Ontario M4P 2Y3, Canada
(a division of Pearson Penguin Canada Inc.)
Penguin Books Ltd., 80 Strand, London WC2R 0RL, England
Penguin Group Ireland, 25 St. Stephen's Green, Dublin 2, Ireland (a division of Penguin Books Ltd.)
Penguin Group (Australia), 250 Camberwell Road, Camberwell, Victoria 3124, Australia
(a division of Pearson Australia Group Pty. Ltd.)
Penguin Books India Pvt. Ltd., 11 Community Centre, Panchsheel Park, New Delhi—110 017, India
Penguin Group (NZ), Cnr. Airborne and Rosedale Roads, Albany, Auckland 1310, New Zealand
(a division of Pearson New Zealand Ltd.)
Penguin Books (South Africa) (Pty.) Ltd., 24 Sturdee Avenue, Rosebank, Johannesburg 2196,
South Africa

Penguin Books Ltd., Registered Offices: 80 Strand, London WC2R 0RL, England

A Perigee Book
Published by The Berkley Publishing Group
375 Hudson Street
New York, NY 10014

Copyright © 1995 by Wendy Reid Crisp
Book design by Joseph Perez
Text illustrations ©1995 by Liz Conrad

This book is an original publication of The Berkley Publishing Group.

First Perigee edition: May 1995
Revised Perigee edition: April 2006

Published simultaneously in Canada.

Library of Congress Cataloging-in-Publication Data
100 things I'm not going to do now that I'm over 50 / Wendy Reid Crisp.—1st ed.
p.   cm.
"A Perigee book."
ISBN 0-399-51936-X
1. Middle age—Humor. 2. Middle aged women—Humor. I. Title. II. Title: One hundred things I'm not going to do now
that I'm over 50. III. Title 100 things I'm not going to do now that I'm over 50.
PN6231.M47C75   1995
818\.5402—dc20

94-24657
CIP

PRINTED IN THE UNITED STATES OF AMERICA

10 9 8 7 6 5 4 3 2 1

For Mil, for the laughter

Thank You

Linda Russ, Pam Mauney, Dennis Mauney,
Ewing Walker, Jill Mason, Evie Righter,
Julie Merberg and Carla Glasser.

Introduction

"Postmenopausal zest," Margaret Mead called it—"it," that surge of exhilarating orneriness we first feel on the cusp of fifty. Almost thirty years ago, I saw the zest flame in Mead as she strode onto the stage at a California university wearing a long, loosely flowing dress over a short, stout body, propelling herself forward with the aid of a six-foot shepherd's crook, to address a crowd of mostly twenty-something women on the challenge of being a courageous, original individual. If Mead is an old woman, I thought, then old women are the crux of the earth's wisdom, strength, compassion, and wit.

Henceforth, I knew what I wanted to be when I grew up and I anticipated it fearlessly. Or, at least, semi-fearlessly; there have certainly been pangs of anxiety when confronted with dowagers less inspirational than Mead—Helen Hokinson's *New Yorker* characters, for example, who searched for hankies in the ample bosoms of their watery silk dresses. I began to keep a list—jottings on backs of envelopes—my resolutions for the second half of life.

Once, when I was seventeen, I wrote that the world seemed vast and green and forever. It still does—even if I have to crinkle up my eyes to blur the sorrows and hum to myself to drown out the strains of despair. That's resolution #101: Don't double-cross your own dreams. The kid who wrote that sentiment paid with her youth for the ticket that got me here, to fifty, to postmenopausal zest, to joy.

—W.R.C.

100 Things
I'm Not
Going to Do
Now That I'm
Over 50

I'm not going to . . .

1. *Repeat myself.*

The early symptoms are simple reprises of favorite phrases. Soon, you notice your audience is beginning to nod and finish your sentences. I'm doing an end-run around this conversation roadblock by ending my sentences with nonsense.

"I woke up at two, and, as hard as I tried, I couldn't get back to—"

"Sleep," says the impatient listener.

"Ohio," I say.

I'm not going to . . .

2. *Be honest about*

my age.

Compulsive truth-telling, an off-shoot of the sexual revolution, was easy to espouse when we were twenty-five. As a lifelong behavior, it's seriously in need of modification.

I'm not going to . . .

3. *Introduce body*

parts as topics of

conversation.

In New England, there's a group of women in their sixties who have been friends for forty years and who meet annually for a long weekend at a good spa. Their first event, on Friday night, is an "organ recital." Everyone recites ad nauseam the state of her organs—heart, uterus, lungs, kidneys—and other anatomical conditions. As it should be, for the rest of the weekend the subject of personal health is taboo.

I'm not going to . . .

4. *Show cleavage.*

If I feel an overwhelming need to wear a halter top or a plunging neckline, I'll confine myself to the garden, where, as ancient fertility symbols, what breasts I may be fortunate enough to keep might productively inspire a nonvisual species.

I'm not going to . . .

5. *Countenance BS.*

Our crapometers should be in near-perfect working order, finely tuned by bosses, teenagers, and assorted marginally employed relatives. After fifty, when the delicate gauge registers in the red zone, we can give audible alerts. Much like the important brooch or the scarf of our younger lives, the BS alert can be a personal trademark. "Bullshit" is too much to the point for everyday use; "pshaw" is impossible to pronounce. My mother says "That's the most ridiculous thing I've ever heard," a phrase that I'll avoid for emotional reasons. One friend says "Interesting"; another mutters something in Portuguese and crosses herself. Although I haven't settled on my trademark scoff yet, to enhance my general elegance I'm phasing out "What a crock."

I'm not going to . . .

6. *Wear a corsage.*

Did Margaret Thatcher ever wear cymbidiums to an economic summit? Has Oprah ever appeared in public with a shoulder full of carnations? Nothing strips power from a woman faster than an honorific bouquet on her bosom. I'll tell the well-meaning presenter that flowers close to my nasal passages activates a fatal allergy. On the way home, I'll drop off the box at a rest home. Someone is always having a birthday.

I'm not going to . . .

7. *Diet.*

Low-carb, low-sodium, low-calorie, low-cholesterol, low-fat, vegetarian, vegan, macro-biotic, high-fiber—who cares? It's all mind over body, and my mind is heartily encouraged by a breakfast of spice gumdrops.

I'*m not going to* . . .

8. *Engage in public*

displays of affection

with my dog.

Viola's utter adoration of her mistress, apparently without cause, will be part of my mystique: It is important no one suspects that she sleeps under the electric blanket and eats Danish butter cookies as a matter of course.

I'm not going to . . .

9. *Join AARP.*

A copy of *Modern Maturity* on the coffee table is as cheering an image as a pair of Jehovah's Witnesses on the doorstep.

I'm not going to . . .

10. *Camp.*

The aroma of bacon sizzling in a pan over an open fire drifts through the pines and beckons me from an early morning river bath. A moment of grace, soon to be eclipsed by cleaning the greasy pan in lukewarm water, shaking ants out of sleeping bags, and twisting an ankle on the gravelly incline down the mountain while the kids race on ahead. And now that they've raced their way through school and into their own family tents, I'll be in a hammock somewhere on a terrace in Costa Rica. *Hasta luega.*

I'm not going to . . .

11. *Divorce.*

There's the old joke about the man and the woman in their nineties who go to a lawyer to get a divorce after seventy years of marriage. "Why now?" the attorney asks. "Why not years ago?" They respond, "We were waiting for the children to die." Divorce is unnecessary after fifty: Move to another room, or, if you can swing it, another country.

I*'m not going to . . .*

12. *Date.*

Should I once again find myself connubially adrift, I'm going to go out to dinner and go on picnics and walk and laugh and talk and make love, but I'm not dating. Sex isn't over, but the prom is.

I'm not going to . . .

13. *Take drugs.*

I didn't do it when I was young and drugs were cheap, so why should I do it now, when ten milligrams of something you used to be able to buy on the street for five dollars is sixty dollars and an insurance claim? I'll eat my greens and hope for the best. (Although a local professor claims that feverfew blossoms boiled into a tea can prevent migraines, and one houseguest, sipping to ward off headaches, reports that they're powerful aphrodisiacs. This, after I stripped out the feverfew to make room for the floribunda.)

I'm not going to . . .

14. *Forget to take*

my hormones.

I didn't mean *those* drugs.

I'm not going to . . .

15. *Wear inconspicuous*

earrings.

The old quizzes in *Glamour* helped us find our beauty type: classic, dramatic, gamin, exotic. In mid-life, we have two choices: tasteful or tacky. I'm opting for borderline floozy—dangling rhinestones, silver coyotes with turquoise eyes, peacock feathers.

I'm not going to . . .

16. *Lose touch with*

former lovers.

The expression is an oxymoron. Old friends are precious; still more precious is someone whose recollections of you intersect in soft focus with their own finest moments.

I'm not going to . . .

17. *Freeze casseroles.*

It's a small step before we begin writing novellas on the labels ("September 7, 1990; Italian Delight; serve with green salad, a crusty loaf, a new Beaujolais"), and our feelings of order and accomplishment are diminished with the actual serving. As we reach advanced age and our taste buds fade, we might not recognize our guests' stifled horror when presented with fossilized fettuccine.

I'm not going to . . .

18. *Wear polyester.*

It clings, it melts, it absorbs odors—and worse—it trivializes the wearer, mocking the graceful, naturally aging woman with its slippery, indestructible gaudiness. I plan to wear clothes that will rot at approximately the same rate I do.

I'm not going to . . .

19. *Wear pastels.*

Do color consultants materialize from behind racks of pantsuits to encourage us to transform ourselves into Easter eggs? Diana Vreeland—jet-black hair and jet-black clothes with a wide red slash for a mouth—didn't look young; indeed, she looked old. She also looked interesting, vital, engaged, confident, dashing, individualistic, important. Lime green and yellow and pale blue and lavender and pink are colors for elementary school graduation dresses. God save me from groups of old women, lumps of pastels, sitting in a row like day-old pastries.

I'm not going to . . .

20. *Accept the label*

"senior citizen."

The worst possible euphemism for old woman, it contains echoes of the French Revolution—or at least the movies about the French Revolution, in which citizens who were not saved by the Scarlet Pimpernel lost their heads. So will we if we allow twenty-six-year-old market researchers to define our lifestyles.

I'm not going to . . .

21. *Ever again refer to my life*

—or anyone else's—

as a "lifestyle."

I'm not going to . . .

22. *Get a permanent.*

Every time I'm ready to succumb to the teensy rollers, I'm going to rent the video of Bette Davis as Elizabeth Regina and remind myself that, *sans* control over the burgeoning British Empire, older women are not attractive with tight knots of thinning hair clinging to their scalps like anemones in the sand.

I'm not going to . . .

23. *Be timid about*

wearing hats.

A remarkable amount of droopy hair and weathered face can be camouflaged under a jaunty canopy.

I'm not going to . . .

24. *Ignore the dentist.*

It's a tried-and-true device to please our inner parent: go to the dentist, promise to floss more often, and keep in mind that periodontal surgery costs more than a week in Cabo San Lucas, and the memories aren't comparable.

I'm not going to . . .

25. *Attend reunions.*

I see the family members I want to see, and the last time my high school class gathered—for our thirty-first reunion—we agreed that we had seen everyone we ever wanted to see as many times as we ever wanted to see them.

I'm not going to . . .

26. *Lighten up on*

the makeup.

Or leave the house without eyebrows. The last vibrant picture of me without makeup—shining eyes, rosy cheeks, peachy skin—was taken when I was ten. "Natural beauty" is, like the Rome beauty, a varietal apple. Inner beauty, of course, is not a fiction: If the corners of our mouths turn down, it doesn't matter what color they are.

I'm not going to . . .

27. *Stop drinking.*

There is a significant difference between a disease and a vice. Unafflicted with the former, I refuse to reform myself of the latter. Who am I to neglect either the order or the advice of Paul when he wrote Timothy to "use a little wine for thy stomach's sake" *before* he told him to "fight the good fight"? Even my grandmother, the founder of the San Jose chapter of the Women's Christian Temperance Union, had a beer every afternoon while she did her tatting.

I'm not going to . . .

28. *Save money.*

The day before she died, at ninety-two, I tried to convince my aunt to go to the hospital. "I can't afford it," she protested. "Yes, you can," I said, "you have insurance, you have that money in the bank." "I can't spend that money!" she said. "I'm saving it for my old age."

I'm not going to . . .

29. *Be untidy.*

I've spent the equivalent of five years of my life looking for car keys, glasses, library books, checkbooks, telephone numbers, and gloves—because I was unwilling to spend the equivalent of one year of my life putting things back where they belong. At this rate, my time account will be overdrawn—and for some obscure rebelliousness that has its roots in being forced to clean my room before I could go out and play.

I'm not going to . . .

30. *Have only one set of*

keys and one

pair of glasses.

On the other hand, let's be realistic.

I'm not going to . . .

31. *Talk like the kids.*

The last time my old roommate telephoned, she said, "Hey, dude," and we both suddenly knew she had entered forbidden territory.

I'm not going to . . .

32. *Sing quietly.*

Bang on the piano, put on those old albums of *Grease*. No amount of aerobics can bring up the adrenaline, increase the circulation, fill the lungs and the soul like a lusty song (to say nothing of your self-esteem when you realize the same mind that forgot to deposit that huge check can recall the words to every number in *Mary Poppins*).

I'm not going to . . .

33. *Be nice.*

Compassionate, loyal, thoughtful, kind, generous, considerate, tolerant, fair—but not nice. Not that I ever was.

I'm not going to . . .

34. *Do needlework.*

Unless I decide to spend my evenings cross-stitching a sampler that reads "Do Not Go Gentle Into That Good Night."

I'm not going to . . .

35. *Kiss little children.*

I've seen *The Three Faces of Eve*, and, yes, the kissee was a corpse. To the untrained eye, however, there's a fine line between dotage and death. Who wants to be responsible for generating a trauma so powerful it produces multiple personalities? I'm confining my kissing to women older than me, men of all ages, and the downy tops of babies' heads.

I'm not going to . . .

36. *Apologize for*

memory lapses.

Obvious confusion is more aging than bizarre eccentricity. Like most middle-aged people, I can remember the birthdays of everyone in my third-grade class, but I forget the fourth item I was supposed to pick up at the grocery or the name of my neighbor's husband, who is standing in front of me waiting to be introduced to the friend I just ran into in the post office whose name I can't remember either. Instead of an awkward old-lady fumble, I'm going to invent names—and places and dates and events—and drop them with confidence, bewildering my listeners and shaking their self-assurance.

I'm not going to . . .

37. *Keep a diary.*

My husband's great-grandfather bequeathed thirty years of personal journals containing such heart-stopping entries as "Took a load of cheese to Hornell" and "At home with wife." Unless we take a page from Anaïs Nin—and lie—the examined life is not worth reading.

I'm not going to . . .

38. *Mistake silence*

for maturity.

Still waters don't run deep. Most of them, stagnant and polluted, don't run at all. We've learned this over the years by spending time and warmth drawing people out only to discover they knew best all along: Those who don't talk have nothing to say.

I'm not going to . . .

39. *Tolerate bigots.*

This includes the classism that assumes the cashier from Costco who wears blue eye shadow couldn't possibly be a friend.

I'm not going to . . .

40. *Get even.*

" 'Vengeance is mine,' saith the Lord," and I say let Him do it. He does it better than anyone—what mere mortal from Nixon's Enemy List could have thought up Watergate?

I'm not going to . . .

41. *Fight back tears.*

Always carry a tiny compact, a few Wash-'N-Dris, and an extra wand of mascara. Cry. The universal soul needs the nourishment.

I'm not going to . . .

42. *Find reasons not to visit*

hospitals, rest homes,

and cemeteries.

May I never succumb to the fears of frailty and mortality. Whatever else I may fall prey to, may I never believe that "She wouldn't want me to see her that way," may I never say "I want to remember him as he was" or "I get so depressed in those places, I'll make her feel worse."

I'm *not going to* . . .

43. *Take my own death*

seriously.

The mastery of three emotions will suffice: grief, for the passing of family and friends; compassion, for the deaths of strangers; and humor, for my own demise.

I'm not going to . . .

44. *Call only when the*

rates are low.

Off-peak conversations are an admirable idea if one can sustain the joy, excitement, love, and appreciation that motivated the connection in the first place.

I'm not going to . . .

45. *Attend meetings.*

"It was moved and seconded that a task force be created to determine the necessity of establishing a permanent committee to discuss and develop proposals pertaining to the issues at hand." Unless we are members of the National Security Council or underground coordinators for the Sanctuary movement, the details of every meeting we ever endured will be edited out of our life story.

I'm not going to . . .

46. *Put on a happy face.*

While a certain degree of overt joviality is appropriate—heaven knows, the world doesn't need another carrier of gloom—the "smile" command is due for retirement. I plan to exercise the power of a flash of anger over a well-composed face. I'm also practicing expressions of wry disbelief, undisguised disgust, and righteous indignation.

I'm not going to . . .

47. *Gossip.*

A terminal disease for which the first symptoms are a suddenly dropped voice, averted eyes, and hand gestures that attempt to conceal the mouth. As the malevolence metastasizes, lips become frozen in a pursed expression and the sufferer is restricted to the company of other victims.

I'm not going to . . .

48. *Tell secrets.*

Our friend may eventually wonder why we don't follow up on the details of her infidelity or her daughter's felony conviction, but this unflattering assumption—that we are hopelessly self-absorbed— is inconsequential compared to the risk of her indiscretions appearing on the Internet.

I'm not going to . . .

49. *Drink coffee from a mug*

that says "You've

been like a mother to me."

Or hang in windows or on walls any commercial sentiment about the warmth of my kitchen or the blessings of my home. If we are incapable of intimate expression, ersatz stained glass as a medium is a damned poor substitute.

I'm not going to . . .

50. *Broker communications*

between friends or

family members.

I will not carry messages between warring factions, translate from the passive, or engage in speculative interpretations—unsolicited or otherwise. If the children have bad news, let them tell Dad directly. The messenger usually gets shot, and once in the conversational loop, we have to listen to both sides rant when we could be using the time to read a book on mysticism or run for Congress.

I'm not going to . . .

51. *Cash unexpected checks.*

Not even a law degree from Harvard can guide us and our bifocals through that entanglement of tiny type that explains, ever so legally, that if we take the money and run, strange credit card debts will follow us to the end of time. And never fear: if you don't have a credit card, one will be provided for you.

I'm not going to . . .

52. *Be accessible 24/7.*

One friend is so compulsive, she responded to the "Hey, Jude" jingle on her cell phone during a fire. "I can't talk right now," she said, "the house is burning." Consider instead the delicious arrogance of Charles de Gaulle, who refused to accept incoming calls. "If I had wanted to speak with him," he said, "I would have called him myself."

I'm not going to . . .

53. *Put "career objective"*

on a résumé.

We may yet be uncertain of what we want to be when we grow up; however, as great-grandmother would have said, "That should be our little secret, dear."

I'm not going to . . .

54. *Buy anything in a chain*

store that could be

purchased from a locally

owned business.

While driving through Indiana one summer, I was listening to the radio when a woman on a talk show said, "My kids are always telling me to shop at the discount stores at the mall. They say, 'You'll get a real bargain there, Mom.' And I say, 'Those people downtown know who I am and who your father was and I've helped them out and they've helped me out for over forty years. I know who I can depend on and who this town can depend on. That's a *real* bargain.'"

I'm not going to . . .

55. *Write down anything*

I don't want read aloud

in court.

An ancient admonition that must be expanded to include emails, blogs, voicemail, faxes, electronic bulletin boards, and home videos. Even in a pristinely legal life, what is written remains: Grandma Robertson's enduring legacy is a bundle of vicious letters accusing dotty Aunt Thelma of concubinage.

I'm not going to . . .

56. *Drive boxy blue*

and gray cars.

Give me trucks, vintage T-Birds, sports cars—anything that doesn't resemble a mid-priced coffin.

I'm not going to . . .

57. *Store possessions that*

could have meaningful lives

with new owners.

We've long tut-tutted about a country that hoards silos of grain and warehouses of cheese when there are people starving on every continent, yet we cut a narrow swath of social responsibility when it comes to those boxes of old blankets in the attic, eight sweaters of the wrong colors (summer, and we're fall), and six Pyrex pie dishes we're hanging on to in case we have ten grandchildren and they all show up some Thanksgiving.

I'm not going to . . .

58. *Stoop.*

A hapless resolution, coming, as it does, from one who has not been able to drink white milk since being weaned; regardless, good posture is less painful than a face-lift and drops twice as many years.

I'm not going to . . .

59. *Be defined by*

the company

I keep.

Now that global warming has screwed up the migratory routes, even birds of a feather don't flock together. Why should we?

I'm not going to . . .

60. *Leave an unmade bed.*

In the same category as wearing ratty underwear, filed under "Mom Was Right."

I'm not going to . . .

61. *Remain monolingual.*

When we trip and fall down the subway stairs, we'll need to be able to communicate with the people who will rush to help us. If we're not sure which language to learn, we can wait to see what our grandchildren will be speaking.

I'm not going to . . .

62. *Miss an eclipse.*

Eighteen solar eclipses will take place in the western hemisphere over the next forty years—and why confine ourselves to one hemisphere? It has occurred to me that the four constellations I can recognize—the Big Dipper, the Little Dipper, Cassiopeia, and Orion—are the same four constellations I learned when I was six. A birthday present to myself: *A Field Guide to Stars and Planets* by Donald H. Menzel and Jay M. Pasachoff (Houghton Mifflin, 1983). Eschatologically, I don't believe the heavens are Heaven; however, a contrarian could argue that the ability to identify only four constellations is like planning to move to New York someday and not bothering to learn the difference between the Village and Staten Island.

I'm not going to . . .

63. *Share a bathroom.*

This is no longer a self-indulgent luxury, and anyway, it's scriptural: Our bodies are temples, and we're told to worship in private.

I'm not going to . . .

64. *Have a joint checking*

account.

No woman over fifty should have to explain why she paid seventy-five dollars for a shower curtain—nor should she be asking anyone else such questions.

I'm not going to . . .

65. *Hesitate to haggle.*

"How much is that beveled glass mirror?" I used to inquire. "Two zillion dollars," the tight-lipped antiques dealer would reply. "Oh, okay, that's fine," I'd say, hurriedly writing the check that was supposed to be my house payment. The mature me says, "For an unsilvered, cracked reproduction?" Then I move on, musing over the china, while the dealer goes behind the curtain, pretends to check with Mrs. Kearns from Greenwich who said she was definitely coming in before ten to buy that mirror for two zillion, and oh, it's ten-fifteen—sixty-five dollars will be fine.

I'm not going to . . .

66. *Wear a plastic rainhat.*

Tuck a hanky in my bosom. Carry a white purse. Have a set of earrings that matches a pin. Leave skirts at off-the-rack length.

I'm not going to . . .

67. *Wake up houseguests.*

Especially if they're my own children. As far as I'm concerned, they can sleep through the tour of the Redwoods or the job interview. Get yourself up or stay at the Marriott.

I'm not going to . . .

68. *Sleep on wrinkled sheets.*

During a brief professional leave of absence, I accidentally ironed pillowcases while listening to "Performance Today." Whether it was the smell of freshly laundered cotton, the softness against my face, or the memory of Chopin's "Polonaise in A-Flat," I experienced a measurable difference in sleep quality. And my dreams! Don't ask.

I'm not going to . . .

69. *Eat cheap ice cream.*

Or drink "lite" beer. Who are we kidding? This is all-or-nothing territory, folks.

I'*m not going to* . . .

70. *Be a snob about*

television.

TV is junk! It's deplorable! The trouble is, everyone seems to have a different definition of junk. Unbelievable as it may seem, there are some people who aren't addicted to *Design on a Dime* and who don't appreciate the sociological nuances of *General Hospital*.

I'm not going to . . .

71. *Bargain with God.*

Never again. He holds us to our promises to the last syllable of recorded time. Better to just talk things over.

I'm not going to . . .

72. *Stop walking.*

For the exercise, and for the rich, detailed world view.

I'm not going to . . .

73. *Neglect friends.*

By now, we have learned a painful lesson at least once: How were we to know that conversation, that letter, that summer visit would be our last?

I'm not going to . . .

74. *Avoid mentioning*

the dead.

Grief is not assuaged by oblivion; wounds are not exacerbated by remembrance. Our immortality may be only in vigorous memories; our healing surely is.

I'm not going to . . .

75. *Suffer gadgetry*

intimidation.

No form of mechanical or technological device, recently invented or simply new to us, should be considered beyond our realm of mastery. Bypassing the difficult erodes self-confidence. Old is to be expected; incompetence is not.

I'm not going to . . .

76. *Be vague on where*

Ghana is.

Or lose track of a couple of South American nations or be familiar with the cultural milieu of only three former Soviet republics.

I'm not going to . . .

77. *Graciously share my*

grandchildren.

Holidays with *her* parents? Over my dead body.

I'm not going to . . .

78. *Devalue housework.*

The secret of female longevity lies in discovering the Zen of vacuuming. I'll never have a floor you can eat on, but these days, thanks to Electrolux serenity, you can *walk* on it.

I'm not going to . . .

79. *Underestimate the*

pleasure of the perfect

hors d'oeuvre.

Since young ladies are no longer trained in the niceties of gracious living, we are offered raw cauliflowerets and pallid strips of zucchini—presumably considered suitable accompaniments to a shot of Jack Daniel's—when everyone over fifty understands that at the end of the day, triangles of spanakopita and a platter of hot wings are nigh Nirvana. There were some profound moral precepts in the Eisenhower era, and the Swedish meatball was one of them.

I'm not going to . . .

80. *Override the afternoon*

window of sleepability.

I am a vision of feline sensuality, stretching languorously on a sun-warmed chaise. I am not a middle-aged woman taking a nap.

I'm not going to . . .

81. *Give up trying to*

appreciate jazz.

Twenty-five years ago, friends started me off in Jazz 101 by bringing over a couple of Miles Davis albums. I did not progress beyond Dave Brubeck's greatest hits, but I keep hoping that in my waning decades I'll understand Coltrane. I'm convinced I'll be a better person for it.

I'm not going to . . .

82. *Tell "real" jokes.*

The kind where two guys and a llama walk into a bar.

I'm not going to . . .

83. *Pass along obscene emails.*

We aspire to be outrageous, individualistic, earthy, sensual, open-minded— far beyond such semiliterate broadcasts. The genre is vulgar, and from vulgarity there is no social redemption.

I'm not going to . . .

84. *Go to Japan.*

It's a long time to sit on a plane to spend ten dollars for a glass of orange juice, and too many people are there already.

I'm not going to . . .

85. *Bathe more often*

than necessary.

When a long, hot soak in the tub has to be followed by $200 worth of oils and creams in order to return to pre-prune condition, you gotta wonder.

I'*m not going to* . . .

86. *Smoke.*

We can sigh over Myrna Loy movies or photographs of postwar Parisian bistros, but we can no longer savor the taste of sweet, untreated tobacco after a fine meal, or give the excuse that, "when a lovely flame dies, smoke gets in your eyes." Alas, what deprivation to be born into this healthy generation.

I'm not going to . . .

87. *Search for past lives.*

Geneticists say we're carrying around DNA from at least twenty former generations, so it's no surprise that we have déjà vu when landing in the Azores or driving through Duluth: A random chromosome from crazy Uncle Cedric triggers a memory of the aroma of *sopas* or the pattern of the sunlight on the snow. That's my theory; plus, I'm on good terms with my subconscious, and if I'd lived before, I'm pretty sure I would have told myself about it.

I'm not going to . . .

88. *Pretend I can hear.*

The next tycoon entrepreneur will be the marketer of designer hearing aids. You heard it here first.

I'm not going to . . .

89. *Stifle the giggles.*

In spite of the number of people who have claimed to have done so, no one has ever died laughing. Maybe if we could keep the hilarity rolling, we would all live forever.

I'm not going to . . .

90. *Feign an interest in*

spectator sports.

Never mind that my neighbor waxes wistful about the Knicks tickets she gave up in the divorce, and my Scrabble partner will suspend play in the middle of a potential triple-word score to watch the Seahawks—I have nightmares about the afternoon I got lost in Sanford Stadium during a Georgia-Tennessee game and found myself surrounded by thirty-five thousand inebriated alumni wearing red and black and screaming "Go, Dawgs!" The only thing missing was Nero, but I did see one guy who looked a lot like Charlton Heston.

I'm not going to . . .

91. *Stay calm.*

"If you can keep your head while all about you are losing theirs," wrote Rudyard Kipling, "you'll be a man. . . ." Exactly. And the reason he's not losing his head is because he's listening to the NBA scores and hasn't heard a word you said. Among the many pieces of bad advice women have been given ("Smile. Be nice. Look pretty.), "Don't panic" is near the top. Panic is nature's way of telling us something is terribly wrong, and so what if our antenna occasionally activates on a wrong signal? Would you rather be embarrassed or dead?

I'm not going to . . .

92. *Make one problem*

into two.

I was reminded of this when I saw my son

break his ATM card while picking the lock of

his dorm room.

I'm not going to . . .

93. *Allow worry or despair*

to mist over gratitude.

My aunt drew the draperies every morning and said thank you for the blessing of the day ahead. Her reward was 33,745 mornings of health and laughter and light-years of starshine in the town's memories.

I'm not going to . . .

94. *Travel without*

extra food.

There are few terrors as stark as pitching about at thirty-three thousand feet in turbulence so strong it prevents the flight attendants from handing out the snack.

I'm not going to . . .

95. *Quit.*

I'm not going to . . .

96. *Dwell in the past.*

Churchill said, "Never ever ever ever ever give up," and Joplin sang, "Freedom's just another word for nothin' left to lose," and somewhere between Winston and Janis is glory.

Occasional clandestine visits to 1973 and 1986 are permissible if brief and not discussed.

I'm not going to . . .

97. *Lecture the young.*

The day we realize that our teenage years are distanced from those of our children by the same time span that separates us from Woodstock, we need to shut up. Or try to.

I'm not going to . . .

98. *Put a La-Z-Boy in*

the living room.

Add a couple of old cats, a bare lightbulb and voilà! the pageantry of a George Booth cartoon. And when did it become acceptable to elevate our legs and vibrate in public?

I'm not going to . . .

99. *Grow up.*

May I be spontaneous, but not impulsive; tenacious, but not obsessive; caring, but not controlling; awed, but not naïve.

I'm not going to . . .

100. *Repeat myself.*

I can't remember why I thought that was important.